Searchlight Books™

What-If Science?

# Could We Harness the Power of Black Holes?

Cynthia O'Brien

Lerner Publications ◆ Minneapolis

Lerner Publications Company
An imprint of Lerner Publishing Group, Inc.
241 First Avenue North
Minneapolis, MN 55401 USA

For reading levels and more information, look up this title at www.lernerbooks.com.

Main body text set in Adrianna Regular.
Typeface provided by Chank.

**Library of Congress Cataloging-in-Publication Data**

Names: O'Brien, Cynthia (Cynthia J.) author
Title: Could we harness the power of black holes? / Cynthia O'Brien.
Description: Minneapolis, MN: Lerner Publications, [2026] | Series: Searchlight books. What-if science? | Includes bibliographical references and index. | Audience: Ages 8–11 | Audience: Grades 4–6 | Summary: "Black holes are filled with energy. Could we someday harness their energy to power life on Earth? Learn how black holes work, and how we might utilize them as energy sources"—Provided by publisher.
Identifiers: LCCN 2025013629 (print) | LCCN 2025013630 (ebook) | ISBN 9798765688960 library binding | ISBN 9798348029166 paperback | ISBN 9798765698068 epub
Subjects: LCSH: Black holes (Astronomy)—Juvenile literature
Classification: LCC QB843.B55 O29 2025 (print) | LCC QB843.B55 (ebook) | DDC 523.8/875—dc23/eng/20250415

LC record available at https://lccn.loc.gov/2025013629
LC ebook record available at https://lccn.loc.gov/2025013630

Manufactured in the United States of America
1 - CG - 12/15/25

# Table of Contents

Chapter 1

# INVISIBLE ENERGY

Imagine a time very far into the future. Scientists have figured out how to get energy from black holes. The whole world, including electricity, batteries, and other power sources, is powered by energy from space. All machines and technology run on this space energy. Rockets and spacecraft have the power to travel far into space. People may visit or even live on other planets.

## What is a Black Hole?

Black holes aren't holes in space. They are areas with very strong gravity, a force that pulls objects together. A black hole's gravity is the strongest in the universe. It pulls in stars, dust, and other space matter.

**A black hole pulls in everything that comes close to it.**

## What is Gravity?

Gravity is a pulling force. Objects attract each other due to gravity. Heavy objects have a stronger pull than lighter objects. When you throw a ball in the air, it falls back down. Earth's gravity is much bigger than the ball's gravity, so it pulls the ball down. Gravity also works across space. It keeps the Moon moving around Earth and the planets moving around the sun.

**Gravity pulls skydivers to Earth.**

Black holes can pull in huge amounts of matter. Matter is anything that takes up space and has mass. This includes Earth and everything on it. Matter is water, humans, and even air. The matter in a black hole is very dense. This means it is packed tightly together. Even tiny black holes have the mass of a much larger thing.

ROCKS, WATER, AND AIR ARE EXAMPLES OF MATTER.

As gravity pulls matter into a black hole, the matter releases energy into space. Could this energy be harnessed, or collected, and used on Earth? Understanding black holes can help scientists to answer this question.

LIGHTS IN A BUSY CITY NEED ENERGY TO POWER THEM.

# Deep Dive

## Parts of a Black Hole

All the mass of a black hole is in its center. Around the black hole is a black space called the event horizon. Once something passes the event horizon, it will be pulled into the black hole. Outside the event horizon, there can be a bright disk of plasma. This is the hot swirl of dust, gas, and other matter that is spinning into the black hole.

**The mass of a black hole is packed into its center.**

Chapter 2

# LOOKING FOR BLACK HOLES

Our galaxy, the Milky Way, may contain one hundred million black holes. There are probably billions more in the rest of the universe. Black holes come in different sizes. The most common are stellar black holes. They are up to twenty times the mass of the sun.

Stellar black holes probably form when massive stars die. Massive stars are much bigger than the sun. When a massive star runs out of energy, it collapses and produces an explosion. This explosion is called a supernova. The supernova causes the leftover matter to squeeze together very tightly. This creates the stellar black hole.

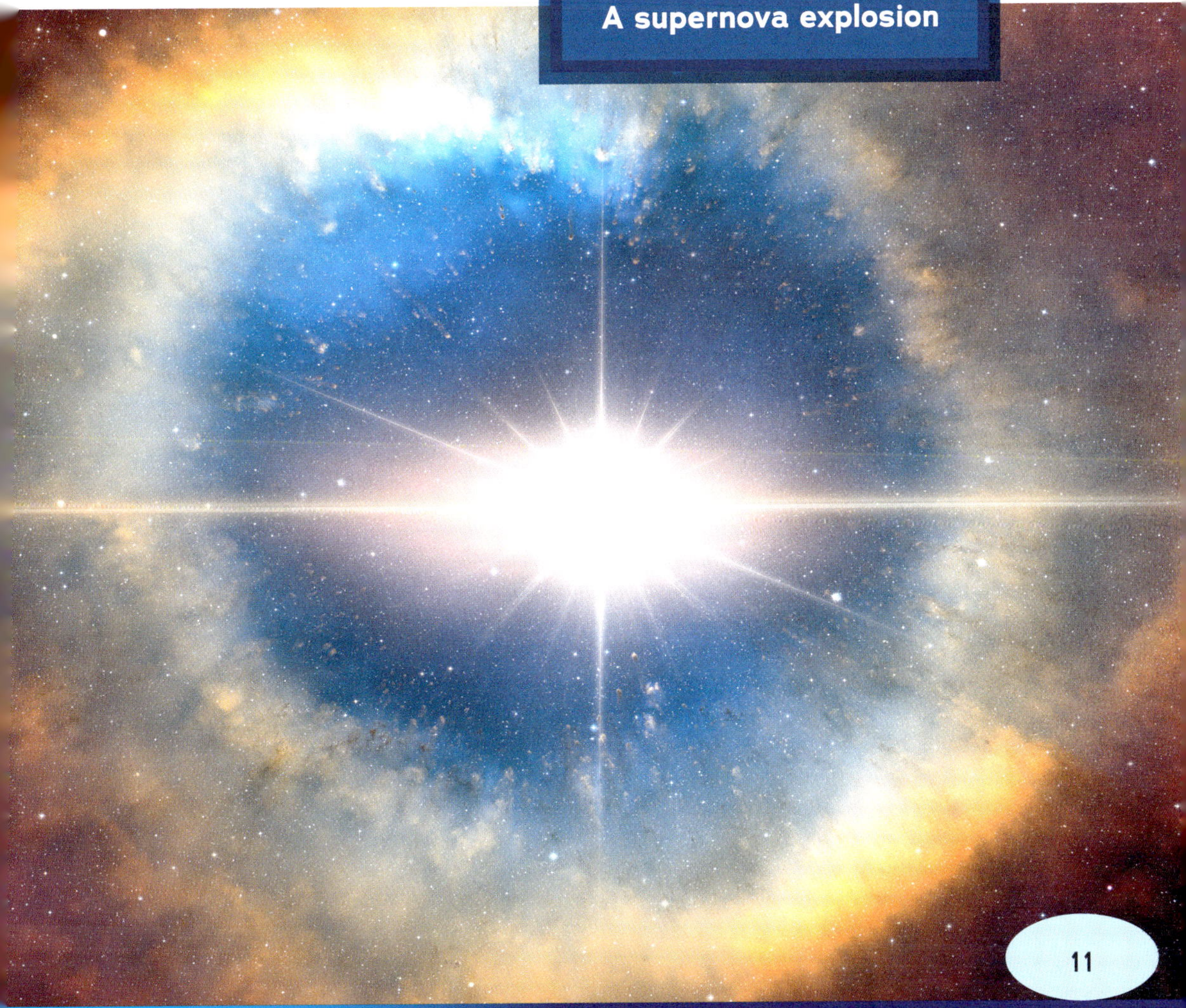

A supernova explosion

This illustration shows a supermassive black hole.

Supermassive black holes are between a million to billions of times larger than the mass of the sun. Supermassive black holes may form from smaller black holes coming together. Ultramassive black holes are the biggest of all. Ton 618 is the largest black hole scientists have discovered. It is more than sixty billion times the mass of the sun.

## Choosing a Name

The first person to write about black holes was English scientist John Michell. In 1783, he thought that black holes could exist, and he named them *black stars*. More than a hundred years later, Albert Einstein wrote about gravity and how it works in space. This was a first step in understanding black holes. In 1964, John Archibald Wheeler was the first to use the term *black hole*. It has been used ever since.

**Albert Einstein wrote about how gravity behaves in space.**

## Finding Black Holes

Black holes are invisible, so how do we know they are there? Scientists look for black holes by seeing how the things around them move. Strong gravity causes stars to orbit quickly around a black hole. The gravity also causes light to bend.

LIGHT THAT PASSES NEAR A BLACK HOLE IS BENT BY THE BLACK HOLE'S GRAVITY.

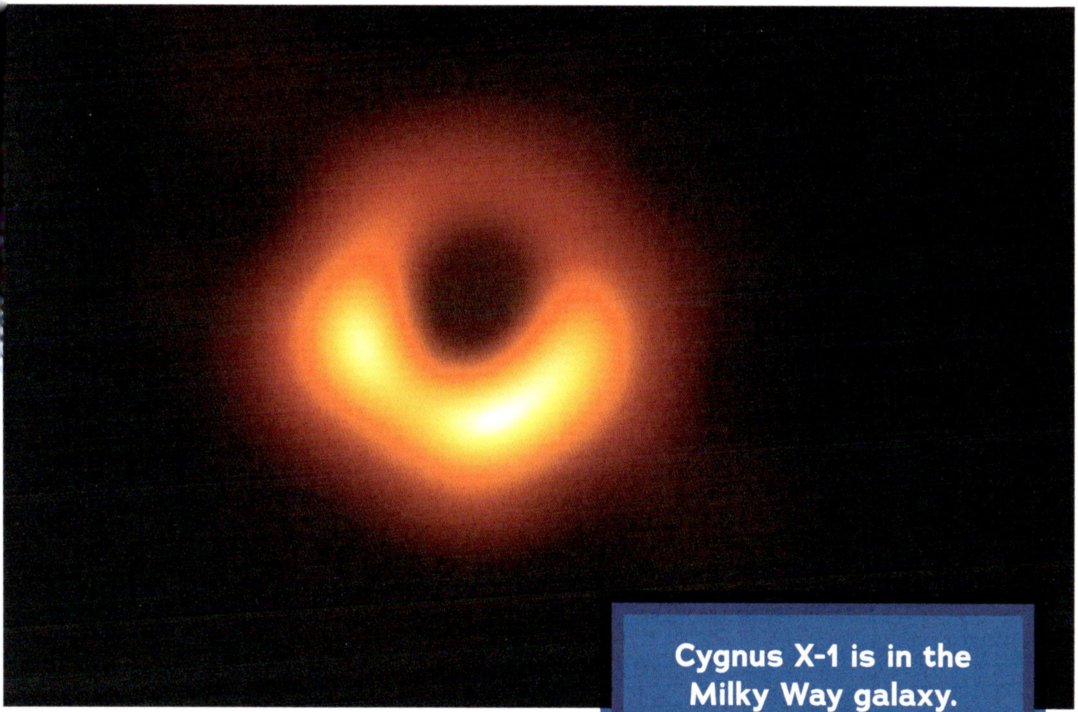

Cygnus X-1 is in the Milky Way galaxy.

Special telescopes can see the rings of plasma that can spin around a black hole. Other telescopes can pick up the energy that these rings give out. The energy comes in invisible radio waves and x-rays. In 1964, astronomers found the first black hole. They sent devices into space that picked up x-rays. The x-rays were coming from a black hole in the Milky Way. Scientists named the black hole Cygnus X-1. Some black holes are hidden by thick clouds and gas. These are not easy to find. Scientists use telescopes that can see heat given off by black holes.

## The First Picture

The Event Horizon Telescope (EHT) is made up of nine space observatories in different sites around the world. In 2019, the EHT took the first picture of a black hole. It showed a hole that is 6.5 billion times more massive than the sun. It is fifty-five million light-years away from Earth. One light-year is 5.8 trillion miles (9.4 trillion km) long. The closest black hole to Earth is Gaia BH1. It is 1,500 light-years away.

This telescope in Spain is part of the EHT.

# Deep Dive

## Sagittarius A

In 2022, the EHT took a picture of a supermassive black hole at the center of the Milky Way. This black hole is called Sagittarius A and it is about four million times the mass of our sun. It is more than twenty-six thousand light years from Earth. Scientists think that most other galaxies also have a supermassive black hole at their center.

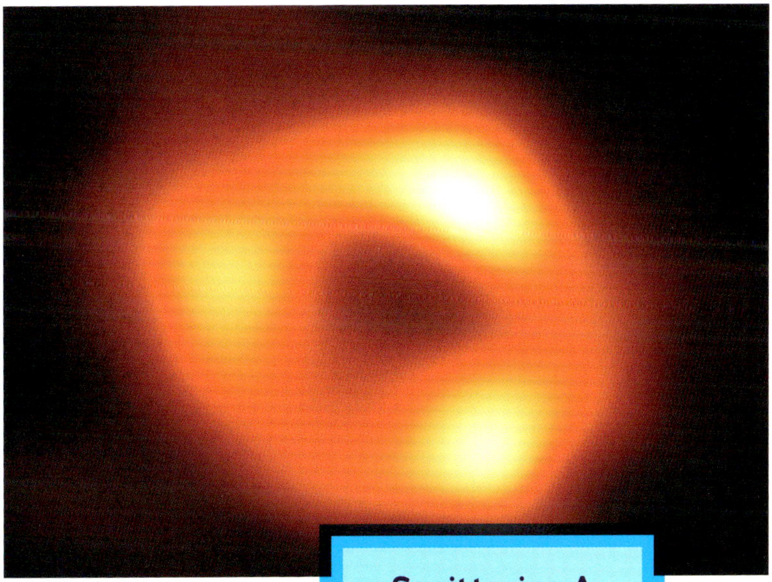

**Sagittarius A**

Chapter 3

# SPACE POWER

All the stars, including the sun, produce energy. The sun's energy is called solar power. People already capture this energy using solar panels. These are devices that collect energy from the sun and turn it into electricity.

Solar panels in space can collect much more energy. Space panels supply power to the International Space Station. This is a large spacecraft where astronauts live and perform experiments. In 2023, scientists tested a device to get solar power from space to Earth. It worked, but only a small amount of energy reached Earth. In the future, scientists may find a way to collect much more solar power. What about other space energy? Is there a way to get energy from black holes and bring it to Earth?

**The International Space Station has large solar panels to generate power.**

## Black Hole Energy

In the 1960s, scientist Roger Penrose suggested that it was possible to get energy from black holes. Penrose's idea was to split the particles around a black hole. One part would go into a black hole and the other would escape. The part that escapes would be charged with energy. Penrose thought that far into the future, people might build the technology to do this.

**Roger Penrose**

THE SUN'S HEAT REACHES EARTH BY RADIATION.

Radiation is heat energy that travels through space. Scientist Stephen Hawking discovered that black holes with smaller mass send out more radiation than those with larger masses. Radiation causes a black hole to shrink.

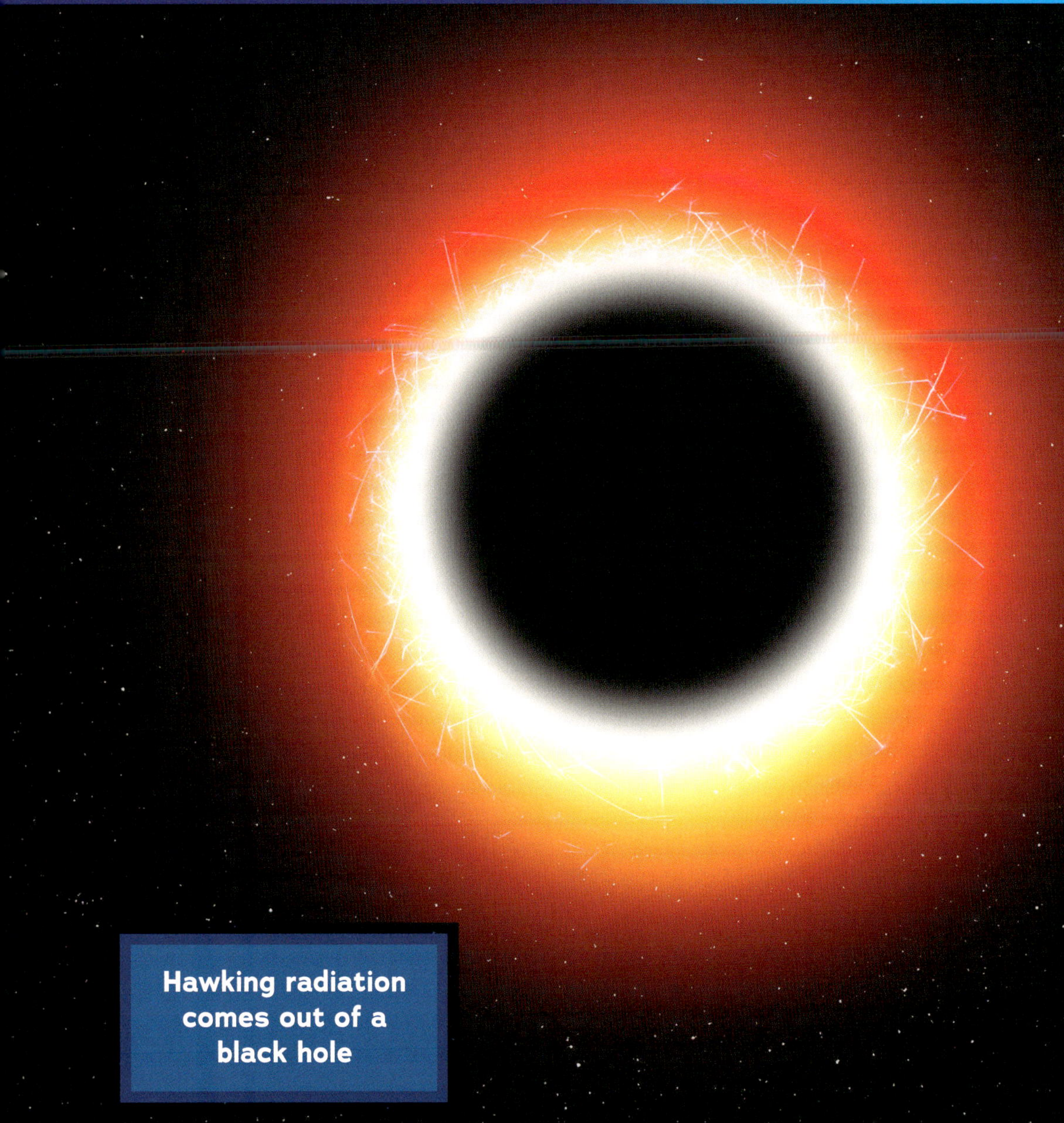

**Hawking radiation comes out of a black hole**

As it shrinks, the black hole sends out more and more radiation. After a very long time, the black hole disappears completely. The radiation from a black hole became known as Hawking's radiation.

## Gathering Energy

How could energy be collected from Hawking's radiation or the black hole's disk? In 1983, scientists George Unruh and Robert Wald suggested that Hawking's radiation could be collected. Some kind of box or device would be lowered near the black hole. The device would gather the radiation energy, like filling a bucket. This could happen again and again until the black hole runs out of radiation.

**Could power be collected from black holes like water from a well?**

Other scientists suggested collecting energy with strings. The strings would be dipped near the event horizon. They would collect the energy there. The energy would travel along the strings to some kind of collection device. This device would transmit the energy back to Earth.

**Energy streams out of a black hole.**

A disk of hot gas and dust spins around a black hole.

## Power Rings

A black hole's greatest source of energy is not inside it. Energy is created as gravity pulls matter into the black hole. The matter does not just fall in. It spins around the black hole as the black hole pulls it in. This creates extremely hot disks of dust and gas. The disks spin around at about 20,000 miles (32,167 km) per second and send out massive amounts of energy into space.

# Spotlight On:
## The Black Hole Initiative

There is still a lot to learn about black holes. The Black Hole Initiative (BHI) in the United States focuses on finding out more. This center brings together scientists and other experts. The BHI hopes to find out more about what lies inside a black hole. They are exploring many other things, too. This includes looking at how black holes affect other things in space.

**The Black Hole Initiative is based at Harvard University.**

## New Ideas

Scientists are still coming up with new ideas about harnessing black hole energy. In 2021, Luca Comisso and Felipe Asenjo built on Roger Penrose's work. Comisso and Asenjo also had the idea of splitting matter. They agreed with Penrose that this could create a lot of energy. Comisso and Asenjo thought that the matter could be made to spin in different directions. This would split the matter up. Some parts would go into the black hole while the others would escape. Spaceships could collect the energy. This may be something that happens in the future.

**In the future, spaceships could carry the power of black holes to Earth.**

Two years later, scientists in China suggested a way of getting energy from very small black holes. Their idea was to feed the black holes with matter. The matter would have an electric charge. This would charge the black holes, like charging a phone battery. The black holes could be recharged again and again. The problem is that these tiny black holes may not exist.

Some scientists think a black hole could be recharged, like a phone battery.

## But What If We Did?

Earth is running out of energy sources such as gas and oil. Burning these fuels also harms the planet. Could black hole energy save the environment? Sending rockets and other spacecraft into space is very expensive. Building technology to travel to black holes could cost billions of dollars. Is it worth it? Would it ever be possible to collect enough black hole energy to power the entire Earth?

# Glossary

**astronomer:** a scientist who studies space

**black hole:** an area of space with such strong gravity that nothing can escape

**energy:** power, such as heat or electricity, that can be used to make something work

**galaxy:** a large group of stars, planets and other matter; the universe contains many billions of galaxies

**harness:** to control and make ready to use

**light-year:** the distance that light travels through space in a year

**mass:** the amount of matter in something

**observatory:** a place with devices to look at space

**orbit:** to move in a circle around an object

**particle:** a very small piece of matter

**plasma:** gas that is so hot that its matter breaks up into electrically charged parts

**technology:** the use of science to solve problems, such as computer technology

# Learn More

Ducksters: Black Holes
https://www.ducksters.com/science/black_hole.php

Goldstein, Margaret J. *Mysteries of Black Holes*. Lerner Publications, 2021.

Green, Joel. *Black Holes*. Norwood House Press, 2023.

Mather, Charis. *Black Holes: Top-Secret Data*. Bearport, 2024.

NASA: What Is a Black Hole?
https://www.nasa.gov/learning-resources/for-kids-and-students/what-is-a-black-hole-grades-k-4/#:~:text=A%20black%20hole%20is%20a,can't%20see%20black%20holes.

*National Geographic Kids:* Black Holes
https://kids.nationalgeographic.com/space/article/black-holes

# Index



# Photo Acknowledgments


Image credits: Archangel80889/Dreamstime, p. 5; vuk8691/iStock, p. 6; by Paul/Shutterstock, p. 7; Mulevich/Shutterstock, p. 8; Tranding art/The Universe001/Shutterstock, p. 9; Muratart/Shutterstock, p. 11; ESA/N. Bartmann/NASA, p. 12; Pictorial Press Ltd/Alamy, p.13; Vadim Sadovski/Shutterstock, p. 14; sameerbro240/Shutterstock, p, 15; Patrick Silveira/Shutterstock, p. 16; EHT Collaboration/ESO, p. 17; Artsiom P/Shutterstock, p. 19; Associated Press/Alamy, p. 20; kenzaza/iStock, p. 21; Science Photo Library/Alamy, p. 22; I am a Stranger/Shutterstock, p. 23; Triff/Shutterstock, p. 24; Nazarii_Neshcherenskyi/Shutterstock, p. 25; Marcio Jose Bastos Silva/Shutterstock, p. 26; Ignatiev/iStock, p. 27; Daniel Krason/Shutterstock, p. 28.

Cover: Elena11/Shutterstock.